History Investigations

The Vietnam War

John Simkin

D1407211

Spartacus (s)

959.7 (s)

Contents

First Published 1987
Spartacus Educational
139 Carden Avenue, Brighton, BN1 8NH

ISBN 0 948865 96 2

Printed by Delta Press, Hove.

Vietnam Chronology

1862	Vietnam becomes part of the French Empire.
1890	Ho Chi Minh is born.
1930	Ho Chi Minh helps to form the Indochinese Communist Party.
1940	Japan occupies Indochina.
1941	Ho Chi Minh helps to organise resistance against the Japanese by forming the Vietminh.
1945	Japan hands over power to the Vietminh. Ho Chi Minh becomes President of Vietnam. Japan surrenders to the Allies. French troops arrive in Vietnam.
1946	War breaks out between France and Vietminh.
1949	Communist victory in China.
1954	France defeated at Dien Bien Phu. Cease-fire agreement signed at Geneva. French troops withdraw from Vietnam.
1955	Ngo Dinh Diem becomes President of South Vietnam.
1956	Diem imprisons Vietminh suspects.
1957	Vietminh start guerrilla war in South Vietnam.
1959	First American military advisers killed in Vietnam.
1960	John Kennedy elected President of the United States. The formation of the National Liberation Front.
1961	Kennedy pledges extra aid to South Vietnam.
1962	American advisers in Vietnam increased from 700 to 12,000. The start of the "Strategic Hamlet" programme.
1963	South Vietnamese army fire on Buddhist protesters. Buddhist monks commit suicide by setting fire to themselves. President Diem is killed during a military coup. President Kennedy is assassinated in Dallas. Lyndon Johnson becomes President of the United States. 15,000 United States military advisers in Vietnam.
1964	North Vietnamese patrol boats fire on American destroyer. Congress pass Tonkin Gulf resolution. American aircraft bomb North Vietnam. NLF attack American air-bases.
1965	Operation Rolling Thunder begins. First United States combat troops sent to Vietnam. 200,000 United States troops in Vietnam.
1966	After a brief pause, Johnson resumes the bombing of North Vietnam. 400,000 United States troops in Vietnam.
1967	Nguyen Van Thieu becomes President of South Vietnam. 490,000 United States troops in Vietnam.

1968	Tet Offensive.
	Major demonstrations take place in America against the war.
	My Lai massacre takes place.
	Johnson announces that he will not run for re-election.
	Peace-talks begin in Paris.
	Richard Nixon elected as President of the United States.
	540,000 United States troops in Vietnam.
1969	Nixon orders secret bombing of Cambodia.
	Start of "Vietnamization" programme.
	Nixon announces troop withdrawals from Vietnam.
	Ho Chi Minh dies in Hanoi.
	480,000 United States troops in Vietnam.
1970	Four student demonstrators killed at Kent State University.
	280,000 United States troops in Vietnam.
1971	Lieutenant Calley convicted of My Lai massacre.
	140,000 United States troops in Vietnam.
1972	Nixon announces mining of Haiphong harbour.
	Nixon re-elected as President.
1973	Cease-fire signed in Paris.
	Last United States troops leave Vietnam.
	United States prisoners of war released.
1974	Nixon resigns over Watergate.
	Gerald Ford becomes President of the United States.
1975	NLF captures Hue and Danang.
	Khmer Rouge takes control of Cambodia.
	Congress refuses to send US troops to Vietnam.
	Thieu leaves Saigon for Taiwan.
	NLF captures Saigon.
	Pathet Lao takes control of Laos.

Historical Background

Vietnam is a small country to the south of China ('vietnamese' means "non-Chinese people of the south"). In 111 BC, Vietnam became part of the Chinese Empire. For the next thousand years Vietnam struggled to gain its independence from its much larger neighbour. This was achieved in 938 AD.

The long period of Chinese rule had left its mark on Vietnam. The language, religion, architecture, system of government and most other aspects of Vietnamese life, reflected the influence of the Chinese.

In the 17th Century, French missionaries arrived in Vietnam. The Catholic priests received a friendly welcome from the Vietnamese people and they were allowed to live and work in the country. However, the Vietnamese authorities became concerned when the missionaries began to recruit the local people to Catholicism. The converted Catholics were told to abandon their religious customs including that of taking several wives. The missionaries also instructed their followers to give their loyalty to God rather than to their Emperor. Hostility towards the Christian missionaries grew and over the years there were several cases of priests being murdered.

In 1847, French troops were sent to Vietnam to protect the Catholic community. News soon got back to France that Vietnam would make a good addition to the French Empire. Nothing was done about it at first but in 1858, Napoleon III sent 14 ships and 2,500 men to the Vietnamese port of Danang. It was a long drawn out struggle but in 1868, the Vietnam Emperor surrendered and signed a peace treaty with France. This did not stop the fighting as China, concerned about the presence of French troops on its border, sent soldiers into Vietnam.

The war continued until 1885, when China finally accepted her inability to defeat the French army and signed an agreement recognising French control over Vietnam. By 1893, the neighbouring states of Laos and Cambodia had also been added to the French Empire.

Vietnam became profitable for the French. Vietnam had good supplies of coal, tin, zinc and rubber. Much of this was sent to France. Vietnam also provided a good market for French manufactured goods. By 1938, 57% of all Vietnam's imports were provided by French companies.

To help transport these raw materials and manufactured goods, the French built a network of roads, canals and railways. To pay for this the French taxed the Vietnamese peasants. This resulted in many peasants being forced to sell their land and seek employment in the new French mines and plantations.

Like the Chinese before them, the French were to change dramatically the Vietnamese way of life. Those who resisted were punished. Others collaborated and agreed to abandon Buddhism and to adopt the Catholic religion and other French customs. In exchange for this sacrifice they were granted privileges in the new Vietnam. This small group, which in time developed into a new elite class, helped the French to control the 30 million people living in Vietnam, Cambodia and Laos, an area that France now called Indochina.

The skills needed by the Vietnamese administrators meant that they would require educating. French schools were built and in 1902, Hanoi University was opened. Although one of the purposes of this education was to develop people who would remain loyal to the French Empire, some students began to question the right of France to rule their country. One such student was Ho Chi Minh.

Ho Chi Minh

Ho Chi Minh was born in 1890. His father, Nguyen Sinh Huy, was a teacher employed by the French. He had a reputation for being extremely intelligent but his unwillingness to learn the French language resulted in the loss of his job.

To survive, Nguyen Sinh Huy was forced to travel throughout Vietnam, offering his services to the peasants. This usually involved writing letters and providing medical care.

As a nationalist, Nguyen taught his children to resist the rule of the French. Not surprisingly, they all grew up to be committed nationalists willing to fight for Vietnamese independence.

Ho Chi Minh's sister obtained employment working with the French army. She used this position to steal weapons that she hoped one day would be used to drive the French out of Vietnam. She was eventually caught and was sentenced to life imprisonment.

Although he had refused to learn French himself, Nguyen decided to send Ho to a French school. He was now of the opinion that it would help him prepare for the forthcoming struggle against the French.

After his studies, Ho was, for a short period, a schoolteacher. He then decided to become a sailor. This enabled him to travel to many different countries. This included several countries that were part of the French Empire. In doing so, Ho learnt that the Vietnamese were not the only people suffering from exploitation.

Ho finally settled in Paris in 1917. Here he read books by Karl Marx and other left-wing writers and eventually he became converted to communism. When in December, 1920, the French

Ho Chi Minh (left) and Giap (right) planning tactics.

Communist Party was formed, Ho became one of its founder members.

Ho, like the rest of the French Communist Party, had been inspired by the Russian Revolution. In 1924, he visited the Soviet Union. While in Moscow, Ho wrote to a friend that it was the duty of all communists to return to their own country to: "make contact with the masses to awaken, organise, unite and train them, and lead them to fight for freedom and independence."

However, Ho was aware that if he returned to Vietnam he was in danger of being arrested by the French authorities. He therefore decided to go and live in China on the Vietnam border. Here he helped organise other exiled nationalists into the 'Vietnam Revolutionary League'.

In September, 1940, the Japanese army invaded Indochina. With Paris already occupied by Germany, the French troops decided it was not worth putting up a fight and they surrendered to the Japanese. Ho Chi Minh and his fellow nationalists saw this as an opportunity to free their country from foreign domination and formed an organisation called the Vietminh. Under the military leadership of General Vo Nguyen Giap, the Vietminh began a guerrilla campaign against the Japanese.

The Vietminh received weapons and ammunition from the Soviet Union, and after the bombing of Pearl Harbour, they also obtained supplies from the United States. During this period the Vietminh learnt a considerable amount about military tactics which was to prove invaluable in the years that were to follow.

When the Japanese surrendered to the Allies after the dropping of atom bombs on Hiroshima and Nagasaki in August, 1945, the Vietminh was in a good position to take over the control of the country.

In September, 1945, Ho Chi Minh announced the formation of the Democratic Republic of Vietnam. Unknown to the Vietminh, Roosevelt, Churchill and Stalin had already decided what would happen to post-war Vietnam at a summit-meeting at Potsdam. It had been agreed that the country would be divided into two, the northern half under the control of the Chinese and the southern half under the British.

The French Indochina War

After the Second World War France attempted to re-establish control over Vietnam. In January 1946, Britain agreed to remove her troops and later that year, China left Vietnam in exchange for a promise from France that she would give up her rights to territory in China.

France refused to recognise the Democratic Republic of Vietnam that had been declared by Ho Chi Minh and fighting soon broke out between the Vietminh and the French troops. At first, the Vietminh, under General Giap, had great difficulty in coping with the better trained and equipped French forces. The situation improved in 1949 after Mao Zedong's communist victory against Chaing Kai-shek in China. The Vietminh now had a safe base where they could take their wounded and train new soldiers.

By 1953, the Vietminh controlled large areas of North Vietnam. The French, however, had a firm hold on the south and had installed Bao Dai, the former Vietnamese Emperor, as the Chief of State.

When it became clear that France was becoming involved in a long-drawn out war, the French government tried to negotiate a deal with the Vietminh. They offered to help set-up a national government and promised they would eventually grant Vietnam its independence. Ho Chi Minh and the other leaders of the Vietminh did not trust the word of the French and continued the war.

French public opinion continued to move against the war. There were four main reasons for this: (1) Between 1946 and 1952, 90,000 French troops had been killed, wounded or captured; (2) France was attempting to build up her economy after the devastation of the Second World War. The cost of the war had so far been twice what they had received from the United States under the Marshall Plan; (3) The war had lasted seven years and there was still no sign of an outright French victory; (4) A growing number of people in France had reached the conclusion that their country did not have any moral justification for being in Vietnam.

General Navarre, the French commander in Vietnam, realised that time was running out and that he needed to obtain a quick victory over the Vietminh. He was convinced that if he could manoeuvre General Giap into engaging in a large-scale battle, France was bound to win. In December, 1953, General Navarre set-up a defensive complex at Dien Bien Phu, which would block the route of the Vietminh forces trying to return to camps in neighbouring Laos. Navarre surmised that in an attempt to re-establish the route to Laos, General Giap would be forced to organise a mass-attack on the French forces at Dien Bien Phu.

Navarre's plan worked and General Giap took up the French challenge. However, instead of making a massive frontal assault, Giap choose to surround Dien Bien Phu and ordered his men to dig a trench that encircled the French troops. From the outer trench, other trenches and tunnels were dug inwards towards the centre. The Vietminh were now able to move in close on the French troops defending Dien Bien Phu.

French soldiers at Dien Bien Phu

While these preparations were going on, Giap brought up members of the Vietminh from all over Vietnam. By the time the battle was ready to start, Giap had 70,000 soldiers surrounding Dien Bien Phu, five times the number of French troops enclosed within.

Employing recently obtained anti-aircraft guns and howitzers from China, Giap was able to restrict severely the ability of the French to supply their forces in Dien Bien Phu. When Navarre realised that he was trapped, he appealed for help. The United States was approached and some advisers suggested the use of tactical nuclear weapons against the Vietminh. Another suggestion was that conventional air-raids would be enough to scatter Giap's troops.

The United States President, Dwight Eisenhower, however, refused to intervene unless he could persuade Britain and his other western allies to participate. Winston Churchill, the British Prime Minister, declined claiming that he wanted to wait for the outcome of the peace negotiations taking place in Geneva before becoming involved in escalating the war.

On March 13, 1954, Giap launched his offensive. For fifty-six days the Vietminh pushed the French forces back until they only occupied a small area of Dien Bien Phu. Colonel Piroth, the artillery commander, blamed himself for the tactics that had been employed and after telling his fellow officers that he had been "completely dishonoured" committed suicide by pulling the safety pin out of a grenade.

The French surrendered on May 7th. French casualties totalled over 7,000 and a further 11,000 soldiers were taken prisoner. The following day the French delegation at the Geneva Peace Conference made it known that they wished to withdraw from Vietnam.

The Geneva Peace Conference

In April, 1954, the foreign ministers of the United States, the Soviet Union, Britain and France decided to meet in Geneva to see if they could bring about a peaceful solution to the conflicts in Korea and French Indochina.

After much negotiation the following was agreed: (1) Vietnam would be divided at the 17th parallel; (2) North Vietnam would be ruled by Ho Chi Minh; (3) South Vietnam would be ruled by Ngo Dinh Diem, a strong opponent of communism; (4) French troops would withdraw from Vietnam; (5) the Vietminh would withdraw from South Vietnam; (6) the Vietnamese could freely choose to live in the North or the South; and (7) a General Election for the whole of Vietnam would be held before July, 1956, under the supervision of an international commission.

After their victory at Dien Bien Phu, some members of the

Vietnam after the Geneva Conference

Vietminh were reluctant to accept the cease-fire agreement. Their main concern was the division of Vietnam into two sections. However, Ho Chi Minh argued that this was only a temporary situation and was convinced that in the promised General Election, the Vietnamese were sure to elect a communist government to rule a re-united Vietnam.

This view was shared by President Eisenhower. As he wrote later: "I have never talked or corresponded with a person knowledgeable in Indochinese affairs who did not agree that had elections been held at the time of the fighting, possibly 80 per cent of the population would have voted for the communist Ho Chi Minh."

United States Involvement in Vietnam

The United States government was severely concerned about the success of communism in South East Asia. Between 1950 and 1953 they had lost 142,000 soldiers in attempting to stop communism entering South Korea. The United States feared that their efforts would have been wasted if communism were to spread to South Vietnam. President Eisenhower was aware that he would have difficulty in persuading the American public to support another war so quickly after Korea. He therefore decided to rely on a small group of 'Military Advisers' to prevent South Vietnam becoming a communist state. Under the leadership of Colonel Edward Lansdale, a twelve-man team of American soldiers and intelligence agents was sent to Saigon in June, 1954. The plan was to mount a propaganda campaign to persuade the Vietnamese people in the south not to vote for the communists in the forthcoming elections.

In the months that followed, this small team of men distributed forged documents that claimed the Vietminh and Chinese communists had entered South Vietnam and were killing innocent civilians. The Ho Chi Minh government was also accused of slaying thousands of political opponents in North Vietnam.

Colonel Lansdale also recruited mercenaries from the Philippines to carry out acts of sabotage in North Vietnam. This was unsuccessful and most of the mercenaries were arrested and put on trial in Hanoi.

Another task of Lansdale and his team was to promote the success of President Diem's rule. Figures were produced that indicated that South Vietnam was undergoing an economic miracle. With the employment of $250 millions of aid per year from the United States and the clever manipulating of statistics, it was reported that economic production had increased dramatically.

Finally, the American advisers set about training the South Vietnamese army (ARVN) in modern fighting methods. For it was

**Colonel Edward Lansdale (second from left)
with Ngo Dinh Diem (centre) in Saigon.**

coming clear that it was only a matter of time before the anti-Diem
forces would resort to open warfare.

Ngo Dinh Diem

Ngo Dinh Diem's ancestors were converted to Christianity by
Catholic missionaries in the 17th Century. Diem, like previous
generations of his family, was educated in French Catholic schools.
After he graduated he was trained as an administrator for the French
authorities in Vietnam. At the age of twenty-five he became a
provincial governor.

During the French-Indochina War, Diem left Vietnam for the
United States. He met influential catholics like Cardinal Spellman of
New York and John F. Kennedy. He told them that he opposed both
communism and French colonialism and argued that he would make
a good leader of Vietnam if the French decided to withdraw.

When the Geneva conference took place in 1954, the United
States delegation proposed Diem's name as the new ruler of South
Vietnam. The French argued against this claiming that Diem was
"not only incapable but mad". However, eventually it was decided
that Diem presented the best opportunity to keep South Vietnam
from falling under the control of communism.

Once in power, the Americans discovered that Diem was
unwilling to be a 'puppet' ruler. He constantly rejected their advice
and made decisions that upset the South Vietnamese people. Several

attempts were made to overthrow Diem but although the Americans were unhappy with his performance as President, they felt they had no choice but to support him.

In October, 1955, the South Vietnamese people were asked to choose between the former Emperor, Bao Dai, and Diem for the leadership of the country. Colonel Lansdale suggested that Diem should provide two ballot papers, red for Diem and green for Bao Dai. Lansdale hoped that the Vietnamese belief that red signified good luck whilst green indicated bad fortune, would help influence the result.

When the voters arrived at the polling stations they found Diem's supporters in attendance. One voter complained afterwards: "They told us to put the red ballot into envelopes and to throw the green ones into the wastebasket. A few people, faithful to Bao Dai, disobeyed. As soon as they left, the agents went after them, and roughed them up... They beat one of my relatives to pulp."

After the election Diem informed his American advisers that he had achieved 98.2 per cent of the vote. They warned him that these figures would not be believed and suggested that he published a figure of around 70 per cent. Diem refused and as the Americans predicted, the election undermined his authority.

The North Vietnamese government reminded Diem that a General Election for the whole of the country was due in July, 1956. Diem refused to accept this and instead began arresting his opponents. In a short period of time, approximately 100,000 people were put in prison camps. Communists and socialists were his main targets but journalists, trade-unionists and leaders of religious groups were also arrested. Even children found writing anti-Diem messages on walls were put in prison.

National Liberation Front

When it became clear that Diem had no intention of holding elections for a united Vietnam, his political opponents began to consider alternative ways of obtaining their objectives. Some came to the conclusion that violence was the only way to persuade Diem to agree to the terms of the 1954 Geneva Conference. The year following the cancelled elections saw a large increase in the number of people leaving their homes to form armed groups in the forests of Vietnam. At first they were not in a position to take on the South Vietnamese Army and instead concentrated on what became known as 'soft targets'. In 1959, an estimated 1,200 of Diem's government officials were murdered.

Ho Chi Minh was initially against this strategy. He argued that the opposition forces in South Vietnam should concentrate on organising support rather than carrying out acts of terrorism against Diem's government.

In 1959, Ho Chi Minh sent Le Duan, a trusted adviser, to visit South Vietnam. Le Duan returned to inform his leader that Diem's policy of imprisoning the leaders of the opposition was so successful that unless North Vietnam encouraged armed resistance, a united country would never be achieved.

Ho Chi Minh agreed to supply the guerrilla units with aid. He also encouraged the different armed groups to join together and form a more powerful and effective resistance organisation. This they agreed to do and in December, 1960, the 'National Front for the Liberation of South Vietnam' (NLF) was formed. The NLF, or the 'Vietcong', as the Americans were to call them, was made up of over a dozen different political and religious groups. Although the leader of the NLF, Hua Tho, was a non-marxist, Saigon lawyer, large numbers of the movement were supporters of communism.

The NLF put forward a ten-point programme. It included the replacement of the Catholic dominated Diem administration with a government that: "represented all social classes and religions."

The most popular aspect of the NLF programme was the promise to take the land from the rich and to distribute it amongst the peasants. During the Indochina War the Vietminh had taken the land

Diem's troops obtain information from NLF suspect

15

from the large landowners in the territory they controlled and given it to the peasants. After Diem had gained power in South Vietnam, he forced the peasants to pay for the land they had been given. This was often more than the peasants could afford and it caused a considerable amount of suffering amongst the peasant community. The promise of the NLF to give the peasants their land free of charge was an important factor in persuading them to help the guerrillas in their fight against the Diem government.

President Kennedy and Vietnam

John F. Kennedy was elected President of the United States in November, 1960. In the first speech he made to the American public as their President, Kennedy made it clear that he intended to continue Eisenhower's policy of supporting Diem's South Vietnamese government. He argued that if South Vietnam became a communist state, the whole of the non-communist world would be at risk. If South Vietnam fell, Laos, Cambodia, Burma, Philippines, New Zealand and Australia would follow. If communism was not halted in Vietnam it would gradually spread throughout the world. This view became known as the 'Domino Theory'. Kennedy went on to argue: "No other challenge is more deserving of our effort and energy... Our security may be lost piece by piece, country by country." Under his leadership, America would be willing to: "pay any price, bear any burden, meet any hardship, support any friend, oppose any foe to assure the survival and success of liberty."

Kennedy's speech had a considerable impact on many young Americans. Philip Caputo was one of those who traced back his decision to join the US Marines to Kennedy's inauguration speech: "War is always attractive to young men who know nothing about it, but we had also been seduced into uniform by Kennedy's challenge to 'ask what you can do for your country' and by the missionary idealism he had awakened in us... we believed we were ordained to play cop to the Communists' robber and spread our own political faith around the world."

When Kennedy became President he was given conflicting advice on Vietnam. Some, like President de Gaulle of France, warned him that if he was not careful, Vietnam would trap the United States in "a bottomless military and political swamp." However, most of his advisers argued that with a fairly small increase in military aid, the United States could prevent a NLF victory in South Vietnam.

Kennedy agreed and in 1961 he arranged for the South Vietnamese to receive the money necessary to increase the size of their army from 150,000 to 170,000. He also agreed to send another 100 military advisers to Vietnam to help train the South Vietnamese

16

A child clings to her father who is an NLF suspect.

army. As this decision broke the terms of the Geneva Agreement, it was kept from the American public.

In 1962, the 'Strategic Hamlet' programme was introduced. For sometime the governments of South Vietnam and the United States had been concerned about the influence of the NLF on the peasants. In an attempt to prevent this they moved the peasants into new villages in areas under the control of the South Vietnamese army. A stockade was built around the village and these were then patrolled by armed guards.

This strategy failed dismally and some observers claimed that it actually increased the number of peasants joining the NLF. As one pointed out: "Peasants resented working without pay to dig moats, implant bamboo stakes, and erect fences against an enemy that did not threaten them but directed its sights against government officials."

In the majority of cases the peasants did not want to move and so the South Vietnamese army often had to apply force. This increased the hostility of the peasants towards the Diem government.

The peasants were angry at having to travel longer distances to reach their rice fields. Others were upset for religious reasons for they believed that it was vitally important to live where their ancestors were buried.

Kennedy became worried when he was informed that despite the 'Strategic Hamlet' programme, the membership of the NLF had grown to over 17,000 - a 300 per cent increase in two years - and that they now controlled over one-fifth of the villages in South Vietnam.

These details were used to pressurise Kennedy into supplying more military advisers. This he agreed to do and by the end of 1962 there were 12,000 in Vietnam. Kennedy also made the decision to supply South Vietnam with 300 helicopters. Their American pilots were told not to become "engaged in combat" but this became an order that was difficult to obey. Although Kennedy denied it at the time, American soldiers were becoming increasingly involved in the fighting in Vietnam.

Buddhism

Roman Catholics made up only just over 10% of the population in South Vietnam. As a reward for adopting the religion of their French masters, Catholics had always held a privileged position in Vietnam. The Catholic Church was the largest landowner in the country and most of the officials who helped administer the country for the French were Catholics.

The main religion in Vietnam was Buddhism. Surveys carried out in the 1960s suggest that around 70% of the population were followers of Buddha. The French, aware of the potential threat of Buddhism to their authority, passed laws to discourage its growth.

After the French left Vietnam the Catholics managed to hold onto their power in the country. President Diem was a devout Catholic and tended to appoint people to positions of authority who shared his religious beliefs. This angered Buddhists, especially when the new government refused to repeal the anti-Buddhist laws passed by the French.

On May 8, 1963, Buddhists assembled in Hue to celebrate the 2527th birthday of the Buddha. Attempts were made by the police to disperse the crowds by opening fire on them. One woman and eight children were killed in their attempts to flee from the police.

The Buddhists were furious and began a series of demonstrations against the Diem government. In an attempt to let the world know how strongly they felt about the South Vietnamese government, it was decided to ask for volunteers to commit suicide.

On June 11, 1963, Thich Quang Duc, a sixty-six year old monk, sat down in the middle of a busy Saigon road. He was then surrounded by a group of Buddhist monks and nuns who poured

The death of Thich Quang Duc

petrol over his head and then set fire to him. One eyewitness later commented: "As he burned he never moved a muscle, never uttered a sound, his outward composure in sharp contrast to the wailing people around him." While Thich Quang Duc was burning to death, the monks and nuns gave out leaflets calling for Diem's government to show "charity and compassion " to all religions.

The government's response to this suicide was to arrest thousands of Buddhist monks. Many disappeared and were never seen again. By August another five monks had committed suicide by setting fire to themselves. One member of the South Vietnamese government responded to these self-immolations by telling a newspaper reporter: "Let them burn, and we shall clap our hands." Another offered to supply Buddhists who wanted to commit suicide with the necessary petrol.

These events convinced President Kennedy that Diem would never be able to unite the South Vietnamese against communism. Several attempts had already been made to overthrow Diem but Kennedy had always instructed the CIA and the US military forces in Vietnam to protect him. In order to obtain a more popular leader of South Vietnam, Kennedy agreed that the role of the CIA should change. Lucien Conein, a CIA operative, provided a group of South Vietnamese generals with $40,000 to carry out the coup with the promise that US forces would make no attempt to protect Diem.

At the beginning of November, 1963, President Diem was overthrown by a military coup. After the generals had promised

If there's an election tomorrow, which general would you vote for?"

Diem that he would be allowed to leave the country they changed their mind and killed him. Three weeks later, President Kennedy was also assassinated.

Gulf of Tonkin

After the assassination of John F. Kennedy, Lyndon Johnson became President of the United States. Johnson was a strong supporter of the 'Domino Theory' and believed that the prevention of an NLF victory in South Vietnam was vital to the defence of the United States: "If we quit Vietnam, tomorrow we'll be fighting in Hawaii and next week we'll have to fight in San Francisco."

Johnson, like Kennedy before him, came under pressure from his military advisers to take more 'forceful' action against North Vietnam and the NLF. The Joint Chiefs of Staff advised Johnson to send United States combat troops to South Vietnam. The overthrow of President Diem had not resulted in preventing the growth of the NLF. The new leader of South Vietnam, General Khanh, was doubtful that his own army was strong enough to prevent a communist victory.

Johnson told his Joint Chiefs of Staff that he would do all that was necessary to prevent the NLF winning in South Vietnam but was unwilling to take unpopular measures like sending troops to fight in a foreign war, until after the 1964 Presidential Elections: "Just let me get elected," he told his military advisers, "and then you can have your war."

As the election was not due for another eleven months, the Joint Chiefs of Staff feared that this was too long to wait. They therefore suggested another strategy that would be less unpopular with the American public as it would result in fewer of the men being killed. For sometime, military intelligence officers working in Vietnam had believed that without the support of the Hanoi government, the NLF would not survive. They therefore advocated the bombing of Hanoi in an attempt to persuade North Vietnam to cut off supplies to the NLF.

Curtis LeMay, the commander of the US air force, argued that by using the latest technology, North Vietnam could be blasted "back to the Stone Age." Others pointed out that "terror" raids on civilian populations during the Second World War had not proved successful and claimed that a better strategy would be to bomb selected targets such as military bases and fuel depots.

Johnson preferred the latter proposal but was aware he would have difficulty convincing the American public and the rest of the world that such action was justified. He therefore gave permission for a plan to be put into operation that he surmised would eventually enable him to carry out the bombing raids on North Vietnam.

'Operation Plan 34A' involved the sending of Asian mercenaries into North Vietnam to carry out acts of sabotage and the kidnapping or killing of communist officials. As part of this plan, it was decided to send US destroyers into North Vietnamese waters to obtain information on their naval defences. On August 2, 1964, the US destroyer, "Maddox" was fired upon by three North Vietnamese torpedo boats in the Gulf of Tonkin. In retaliation, "Maddox" fired back and hit all three, one of which sank. The "Maddox" then retreated into international waters but the next day it was ordered to return to the Gulf of Tonkin.

Soon after entering North Vietnamese waters, Captain Herrick reported that he was under attack. However, later he sent a message that raised doubts about this: "Review of action makes reported contacts and torpedoes fired appear doubtful. Freak weather reports and over-eager sonar men may have accounted for many reports. No actual sightings by "Maddox". Suggest complete evaluation before further action."

Johnson now had the excuse he had been waiting for and ignored Captain Herrick's second message. He ordered the bombing of four North Vietnamese torpedo-boat bases and an oil-storage depot that had been planned three months previously.

President Johnson then went on television and told the American people that: "Repeated acts of violence against the armed forces of the United States must be met not only with alert defence, but with a positive reply. That reply is being given as I speak tonight."

The Congress approved Johnson's decision to bomb North Vietnam and passed what has become known as the "Gulf of Tonkin" resolution by the Senate by 88 votes to 2 and in the House of Representatives by 416 to 0. This resolution authorised the President to take all necessary measures against Vietnam and the NLF.

Johnson's belief that the bombing raid on North Vietnam in August, 1964, would persuade Ho Chi Minh to cut off all aid to the NLF was unfounded. In the run-up to the November election, the NLF carried out a series of attacks and only two days before the election, the US air base near Saigon was mortared and four Americans were killed.

Barry Goldwater, the right-wing Republican candidate for the presidency, called for an escalation of the war against the North Vietnamese. In comparison to Goldwater, Johnson was seen as the 'peace' candidate. People feared that Goldwater would send troops to fight in Vietnam. Johnson, on the other hand, argued that he was not willing: "to send American boys nine or ten thousand miles away from home to do what Asian boys ought to be doing for themselves."

In the election of November, 1964, the voters decided to reject Goldwater's aggressive policies against communism and Johnson won a landslide victory. What the American public did not know was that President Johnson was waiting until the election was over before carrying out the policies that had been advocated by his Republican opponent, Barry Goldwater.

Escalating the War

Three months after being elected president, Lyndon Johnson launched 'Operation Rolling Thunder'. Unlike the single bombing raid in August 1964, this time the raids were to take place on a regular basis. The plan was to destroy the North Vietnam economy and to force her to stop helping the guerrilla fighters in the south. Bombing was also directed against territory controlled by the NLF in South Vietnam. The plan was for 'Operation Rolling Thunder' to last for eight weeks but it lasted for the next three years. In that time, the US dropped 1 million tons of bombs on Vietnam.

The response of the NLF to 'Rolling Thunder' was to concentrate its attacks on the US air bases in South Vietnam. General Westmoreland, the person in charge of the military advisers in Vietnam, argued that his 23,000 men were unable to defend adequately the US air bases and claimed that without more soldiers, the NLF would take over control of South Vietnam.

On March 8, 3,500 US marines arrived in South Vietnam. They

**American pilot Commander George Jacobson,
following an air raid on North Vietnam in 1965.**

were the first 'official' US combat troops to be sent to the country. This dramatic escalation of the war was presented to the American public as being a short-term measure and did not cause much criticism at the time. A public opinion poll carried out that year indicated that nearly 80% of the American public supported the bombing raids and the sending of combat troops to Vietnam.

Guerrilla Warfare

The term 'guerrilla' originates from the actions of small bands of Spanish soldiers who fought against Napolean's French army in the Peninsular War (1807-1814). The word 'guerrilla' is Spanish for "little war".

The tactics employed by "guerrillas" date back to the ideas of Sun Tzu, the Chinese military strategist who lived over 2000 years ago. Sun Tzu argued that all warfare involves the employing of one's strength to exploit the weakness of the enemy. In his book, 'The Art of War", Sun Tzu gives several suggestions on how to defeat an enemy that is larger and better equipped than your own army.

Sun Tzu's ideas were successfully adapted by Mao Zedong, the leader of the communist forces in China. The establishment of a communist government in China was an inspiration to all revolutionaries in South East Asia. This was especially true of

China's neighbour, Vietnam.

The strategy and tactics of the NLF were very much based on those used by Mao Zedong in China. The NLF was organised into small groups of between three to ten soldiers. These groups were called cells. These cells worked together but the knowledge they had of each other was kept to the bare minimum. Therefore, when a guerrilla was captured and tortured, his confessions did not do too much damage to the NLF.

The initial objective of the NLF was to gain the support of the peasants living in the rural areas. According to Mao Zedong, the peasants were the sea in which the guerrillas needed to swim: "without the constant and active support of the peasants... failure is inevitable."

When the NLF entered a village they obeyed a strict code of behaviour. All members were issued with a series of 'directives'. These included: " (1) Not to do what is likely to damage the land and crops or spoil the houses and belongings of the people; (2) Not to insist on buying or borrowing what the people are not willing to sell or lend; (3) Never to break our word; (4) Not to do or speak what is likely to make people believe that we hold them in contempt; (5) To help them in their daily work (harvesting, fetching firewood, carrying water, sewing, etc.)."

US soldier guards NLF suspects

Most peasants in South Vietnam were extremely poor. For centuries, the Vietnamese peasants had accepted this state of affairs because they believed that poverty was a punishment for crimes committed by their ancestors. The NLF educated the peasants in economics and explained how poverty was the result of the landowner's selfishness. They pointed out that fifty per cent of the agricultural land in South Vietnam was owned by only two and a half per cent of the population. Two thirds of the peasants owned no land at all and were therefore forced to work for the rich landlords.

The NLF's solution to this problem was to take the property of the large landowners and distribute it amongst the peasants. In some cases, the landowners were executed as a punishment for the way they had treated the peasants in the past.

In return for the land they had been given, the peasants agreed to help the NLF by feeding and hiding them. In some cases, the peasants also agreed to take up arms with the NLF and help 'liberate' other villages.

The peasants were motivated by fear as well as a sense of gratitude. The NLF told them that if the US marines or ARVN managed to gain control of the village, they would take the land back. Given this situation, it is not surprising that the peasants saw the NLF as their friends and the US Marines/ARVN as the enemy.

This view was re-inforced if the NLF left the village to escape advancing US or South Vietnamese troops. In an effort to discover information about the NLF, the peasants were sometimes tortured. If evidence was found of the NLF being in the village, the people were punished. As William Ehrhart, a US marine explained: "... they'd be beaten pretty badly, maybe tortured. Or they might be hauled off to jail, and God knows what happened to them. At the end of the day, the villagers would be turned loose. Their homes had been wrecked, their chickens killed, their rice confiscated - and if they weren't pro-Vietcong before we got there, they sure as hell were by the time we left."

As well as taking over the running of villages, the NLF would send out patrols into government controlled areas. The tactics they employed have been described by Robert Taber, who fought with the guerrillas in Cuba, as the war of the flea: "The flea bites, hops, and bites again, nimbly avoiding the foot that would crush him. He does not seek to kill his enemy at a blow, but to bleed him and feed on him, to plague and bedevil him... All this requires time. Still more time is required to breed more fleas... the military enemy suffers the dog's disadvantages: too much to defend; too small and agile an enemy to come to grips with."

To defeat the more powerful enemy, the guerrilla needs to dictate the terms of warfare. In the words of Mao Zedong: "The enemy advances, we retreat; the enemy camps, we harass; the enemy tires, we attack; the enemy retreats, we pursue."

The NLF was told not to go into combat unless it outnumbered the enemy and was certain of winning. It therefore concentrated on attacking small patrols or poorly guarded government positions. To increase its advantage, the NLF relied heavily on night attacks.

At first the NLF used hand-made weapons such as spears, daggers and swords. However, over a period of time, it built up a large supply of captured weapons. A US army survey of weapons in 1964 discovered that 90% of weapons taken from the NLF had previously belonged to the ARVN and the US army.

The NLF also employed booby traps against US and South Vietnamese troops. These took the form of sharpened bamboo staves and fragmentation mines. The most feared mine was the 'Bouncing Betty'. As one marine reported, every step created tension. You constantly asked yourself: "Should you put your foot to that flat rock or the clump of weeds to its rear... The moment-to-moment, step-by-step decision-making preys on your mind. The effect is sometimes paralysis." As another pointed out: "The infantryman knows that any moment the ground he is walking on can erupt and kill him; kill him if he's lucky. If he's unlucky, he will be turned into a blind, deaf, emasculated, legless shell."

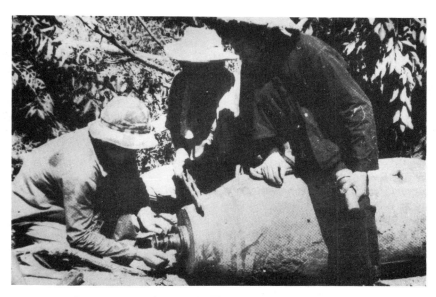

**Members of the NLF extract the explosive
from an unexploded US bomb**

26

Ironically, most of the explosives used for these mines came from unexploded bombs dropped by the United States. It has been estimated that 800 tons of bombs dropped on Vietnam every month failed to explode. These materials were then used to make booby traps.

After seeing their comrades killed by booby traps, there was a temptation for the patrol to take it out on the next village they arrived at. By doing so they increased the peasants hostility towards the Americans and made it more difficult for them to support the South Vietnamese government against the communists.

In 1965, General Westmoreland developed the aggressive strategy of 'search and destroy'. The objective was to find and then kill members of the NLF. The US soldiers found this difficult. As one marine captain explained: "You never knew who was the enemy and who was the friend. They all looked alike. They all dressed alike." Innocent civilians were often killed by mistake. As one Marine officer admitted they "were usually counted as enemy dead, under the unwritten rule 'If he's dead and Vietnamese, he's VC'."

In the villages they controlled, the NLF often built underground tunnels. These tunnels led out of the villages into the jungle. They also contained caverns where they stored their printing presses, surgical instruments and the equipment for making booby traps and land mines. If US patrols arrived in the village unexpectedly, the NLF would hide in these underground caverns. Even if the troops found the entrance to the tunnels, they could not go into the tunnels as they were often too small for the much larger American soldiers.

The overall strategy of guerrilla warfare is to involve the enemy in a long-drawn out war. The aim is to wear down gradually the much larger and stronger enemy. It is only when all the rural areas are under their control and they are convinced that they outnumber the opposition, that the guerrillas come out into the open and take part in conventional warfare. Thus the NLF, who were based in the thick forests of South Vietnam, began by taking control of the villages in the rural areas. As their strength grew and the enemy retreated, they began to take the smaller towns.

Ho Chi Minh Trail

The Ho Chi Minh Trail was a complex web of different jungle paths that enabled communist troops to travel from North Vietnam to areas close to Saigon. It has been estimated that the NLF received sixty tons of aid per day from this route. Most of this was carried by porters. Occasionally bicycles and ponies would also be used.

At regular intervals along the route the NLF built base camps. As well as providing a place for them to rest, the base camps provided medical treatment for those who had been injured or had fallen ill on the journey.

In the early days of the war it took six months to travel from North Vietnam to Saigon on the Ho Chi Minh Trail. But the more people who travelled along the route the easier it became. By 1970, fit and experienced soldiers could make the journey in six weeks.

From the air the Ho Chi Minh Trail was impossible to identify and although the US airforce tried to destroy this vital supply line by heavy bombing, they were unable to stop the constant flow of men and supplies. The main danger to the people who travelled on the Ho Chi Minh Trail was not American bombs but diseases like malaria. In the early days, as many as 10 per cent of the porters travelling down the trail died of disease.

The North Vietnamese also used the Ho Chi Minh Trail to send soldiers to the south. At times, as many as 20,000 soldiers a month came from Hanoi in this way. In an attempt to stop this traffic, it was suggested that a barrier of barbed-wire and minefields called the "McNamara Line" should be built. This plan was abandoned in 1967 after repeated attacks by the NLF on those involved in constructing this barrier.

The Devastation of Vietnam

As the United States is the most advanced industrial nation in world it was able to make full use of the latest developments in technology in its war against North Vietnam.

B-52 bombers, that could fly at heights that prevented them being seen or heard, dropped 8 million tons of bombs on Vietnam between 1965 and 1973. This was over three times the amount of bombs dropped throughout the whole of the Second World War and worked out at approximately 300 tons for every man, woman and child living in Vietnam.

As well as explosive bombs the US air force dropped a considerable number of incendiary devices. The most infamous of these was napalm, a mixture of petrol and a chemical thickner which produces a tough sticky gel that attaches itself to the skin. The igniting agent, white phosphorus, continues burning for a considerable amount of time. A reported three quarters of all napalm victims in Vietnam were burned through to the muscle and bone (fifth degree burns). The pain caused by the burning is so traumatic that it often causes death.

The US also made considerable use of anti-personnel bombs. The pineapple bomb was made up of 250 metal pellets inside a small canister. Gloria Emerson, a reporter in Vietnam, witnessed their use: "An American plane could drop a thousand pineapples over an area

Vietnamese child burnt by napalm

the size of four football fields. In a single air strike two hundred and fifty thousand pellets were spewed in a horizontal pattern over the land below, hitting everything on the ground."

The United States also experimented with the use of plastic rather than metal needles and pellets in their anti-personnel bombs. The advantage of plastic was they could not be identified by X-Ray machines. Dropped on highly populated areas, anti-personnel bombs could severely disrupt the functioning of North Vietnam. It has been claimed that the major objective of the US bombing raids on North Vietnam was not to kill its 17 million population but to maim them. As was pointed out at the time, serious injury is more disruptive than death as people have to be employed to look after the injured where they only have to bury the dead.

One of the major problems of the US forces was the detection of the NLF hiding in the forests of Vietnam. In 1962, President Kennedy approved 'Operation Ranch Hand'. This involved the spraying of chemicals from the air in an attempt to destroy the NLF hiding places. In 1969 alone, 'Operation Ranch Hand' destroyed 1,034,300 hectares of forest. 'Agent Orange', the chemical used in this defoliation programme not only destroyed trees but caused chromosomal damage in people.

Chemicals were also sprayed on crops. Between 1962 and 1969, 688,000 agricultural acres were sprayed with a chemical called 'Agent Blue'. The aim of this exercise was to deny food to the NLF. However, research suggests that it was the civilian population who suffered most from the poor rice harvests that followed the spraying.

In economic terms, the bombing hurt the economy of the United States more than North Vietnam. By the beginning of 1968, it was estimated that $300 million of damage had been done to North Vietnam. However, in the process, 700 US aircraft, valued at $900 million had been shot down. When all factors were taken into consideration it was argued that it cost the United States "ten dollars for every dollar's worth of damage inflicted."

US Troops in Vietnam

Three million US soldiers served in Vietnam between 1965 and 1973. Only about a quarter of these were involved in direct combat with the NLF. The majority were employed in supplying the needs of the combat troops. However, because of guerrilla warfare, there were no 'front-lines' and most Americans in Vietnam came under attack from the NLF at some time during their stay in the country.

The US army drafted (called-up) soldiers at the age of eighteen. To protect them from the stress of war, draftees served in Vietnam for just over a year. As victory did not appear to be in sight, surviving this period became the soldiers' main objective. As one marine explained: "You developed a survival mentality. You stop thinking about what you're doing, and you count days. I knew I was in Vietnam for three hundred and ninety-five days, and if I was still alive at the end of those three hundred and ninety-five days, I'd go home and forget the whole thing. That was the way you operated."

Not all young men in America were drafted. There were several ways that men could avoid being sent to Vietnam. The most popular way was to go to college. As a consequence of this, most soldiers who went to Vietnam came from working, rather than middle-class homes. Ethnic minorities were also more likely to serve in Vietnam than white Americans.

The average age of the soldier fighting in Vietnam was nineteen. Given the nature of the war being fought, these young soldiers were vulnerable to psychological damage. It has been estimated that 700,000 of the soldiers who served in Vietnam have since suffered from some form of stress disorder. According to figures published by the Washington State Department for Veteran Affairs, over 100,000 of these soldiers have committed suicide since returning from the Vietnam War.

The fear of death or serious injury was a constant cause of concern. The belief that the NLF would torture captured US soldiers was another factor in creating stress amongst combat troops.

One of the main problems for the American soldier serving in Vietnam was caused by the climate (an average daily temperature of 27C). Philip Caputo, a Marine officer, argued: "The climate of Indochina does not lend itself to conventional standards of measurement... The only valid measurement was what the heat could do to a man, and what it could do was simple enough: it could kill him, bake his brains, or wring the sweat out of him until he dropped from exhaustion... Relief came only at night, and night always brought swarms of malarial mosquitoes... Mosquito netting and repellents proved ineffective against the horde of flying, creeping, crawling, buzzing, biting things that descended on us... By midnight, my face and hands were masses of welts."

Combat troops also complained about some of the military decisions made by their officers. One of the most controversial battles that took place during the Vietnam War was the one fought for 'Hamburger Hill'. For ten days 600 men attempted to take this hill from the NLF. By the time they had obtained their objective, 476 of the US troops had been killed or wounded. After holding the hill for a day, Lieutenant-Colonel Weldon Honeycutt, the commander responsible for the operation, ordered the men to withdraw.

US soldiers were so angry about these unnecessary deaths that money was raised to pay for the assassination of Honeycutt. Shortly after the assault on 'Hamburger Hill', the soldiers' underground newspaper in Vietnam offered a $10,000 bounty on Honeycutt. Despite several attempts on his life, Honeycutt survived.

It has been admitted that between 1969 and 1971 there were 730 attempts by US soldiers to kill unpopular officers, of which 83 were successful. However, these figures only take into account the cases that were reported and investigated. It has been estimated that the actual figures were very much higher than this.

The Tet Offensive

In September, 1967, the NLF launched a series of attacks on American garrisons. General Westmoreland, the commander of US troops in Vietnam, was delighted. Now at last the NLF was engaging in open combat. At the end of 1967, Westmoreland was able to report that the NLF had lost 90,000 men. He told President Johnson that the NLF would be unable to replace such numbers and that the end of the war was in sight.

Every year on the last day of January, the Vietnamese paid tribute to dead ancestors. In 1968, unknown to the Americans, the NLF celebrated the Tet New Year festival two days early. For on the evening of 31st January, 1968, 70,000 members of the NLF launched a surprise attack on more than a hundred cities and towns in Vietnam. It was now clear that the purpose of the attacks on the US garrisons in September had been to draw out troops from the cities.

The NLF even attacked the US Embassy in Saigon. Although they managed to enter the Embassy grounds and kill five US marines, the NLF was unable to take the building. However, they had more success with Saigon's main radio station. They captured the building and although they only held it for a few hours, the event shocked the self-confidence of the American people. In recent months they had been told that the NLF was close to defeat and now they were strong enough to take important buildings in the capital of South Vietnam. Another disturbing factor was that even with the large losses of 1967, the NLF could still send 70,000 men into battle.

The Tet Offensive proved to be a turning point in the war. In military terms it was a victory for the US forces. An estimated 37,000 NLF soldiers were killed compared to 2,500 Americans. However, it illustrated that the NLF appeared to have inexhaustible supplies of men and women willing to fight for the overthrow of the South Vietnamese government. In March, 1968, President Johnson

NLF suspect executed in Saigon during Tet Offensive

was told by his Secretary of Defence that in his opinion the US could not win the Vietnam War and recommended a negotiated withdrawal. Later that month, President Johnson told the American people on national television that he was reducing the air-raids on North Vietnam and intended to seek a negotiated peace.

The Vietnam Protest Movement

When the Vietnam War started only a small percentage of the American population opposed the war. Those who initially objected to the involvement in Vietnam fell into three broad categories: people with left-wing political opinions who wanted an NLF victory; pacifists who opposed all wars; and liberals who believed that the best way of stopping the spread of communism was by encouraging democratic, rather than authoritarian governments.

The first march to Washington against the war took place in December, 1964. Only 25,000 people took part but it was still the largest anti-war demonstration in American history.

As the war continued, more and more Americans turned against it. People were particularly upset by the use of chemical weapons such as napalm and agent orange. In 1967, a group of distinguished academics under the leadership of Bertrand Russell, set up the 'International War Crimes Tribunal'. After interviewing many witnesses, they came to the conclusion that the United States was guilty of using weapons against the Vietnamese that were prohibited by international law. The United States armed forces were also found guilty of torturing captured prisoners and innocent civilians. The Tribunal, and other critics of the war, claimed that the US behaviour in Vietnam was comparable to the atrocities committed by the Nazis in Europe during the Second World War.

In November, 1965, Norman Morrison, a Quaker from Baltimore, followed the example of the Buddhist monk, Thich Quang Duc, and publically burnt himself to death. In the weeks that were to follow, two other pacifists, Roger La Porte and Alice Herz, also immolated themselves in protest against the war.

The decision to introduce conscription for the war increased the level of protest, especially amongst young men. To keep the support of the articulate and influential members of the middle class, students were not called up. However, students throughout America still protested at what they considered was an attack on people's right to decide for themselves whether they wanted to fight for their country.

In 1965, David Miller publically burnt his draft card (call-up notice) and was sentenced to two and a half years in prison. His actions inspired others and throughout America, 'Anti-Vietnam War' groups organised meetings where large groups of young men burnt their draft cards.

Between 1963 and 1973, 9,118 men were prosecuted for refusing to be drafted into the army. The most famous of these was Muhammad Ali, the world heavyweight boxing champion.

Muhammad Ali was one of the many distinguished black figures who protested against the war. There were several reasons why blacks and other ethnic minorities felt so strongly about Vietnam. One reason involved the expense of the war. By 1968, the Vietnam War was costing 66 million dollars a day. As a result, President Johnson increased income taxes and cut back on his programme to deal with poverty. The blacks, who suffered from poverty more than most other groups in America, were understandably upset by this decision. Martin Luther King, the Civil Rights leader, argued: "that America would never invest the necessary funds or energies in rehabilitation of its poor as long as Vietnam continued to draw men and skills and money like some demonic, destructive suction tube."

Other Civil Rights leaders pointed out that because of the draft deferment enjoyed by college students, it was the poor who were more likely to be sent to Vietnam. What is more, as Eldridge Cleaver, a Civil Rights activist pointed out, in many southern states of America, blacks were being denied the right to vote in elections. Therefore, blacks were fighting in Vietnam "for something they don't have for themselves." As another black leader put it: "If a

ARVN search the village of Ba Gia.

black man is going to fight anywhere, he ought to be fighting in Mississippi" and other parts of America.

This advice was taken and in the late 1960s, several cities in the United States suffered violent riots in black ghettos. 'Anti-Vietnam War' leaders began to claim that if the government did not withdraw from the war they might need the troops to stop a revolution taking place in America.

Demonstrations against the war steadily increased in size during the late 1960s. In New York, over a million people took part in one demonstration. The public opinion polls showed that a narrow majority of the people still supported US involvement in Vietnam. However, the polls also indicated that much of this support came from middle class families whose own sons were not at risk. President Johnson knew that if the war continued, he would eventually be forced to start drafting college students. When that happened he would have great difficulty obtaining majority support for the war.

The most dramatic opposition to the war came from the soldiers themselves. Between 1960 and 1973, 503,926 members of the US armed forces deserted. Many soldiers began to question the morality of the war once they began fighting in Vietnam. One soldier, Keith Franklin, wrote a letter that was only to be opened on his death. He was killed on May 12, 1970:

"If you are reading this letter, you will never see me again, the reason being that if you are reading this I have died. The question is whether or not my death has been in vain. The answer is yes.

The war that has taken my life and many thousands before me is immoral, unlawful and an atrocity... I had no choice as to my fate. It was predetermined by the war-mongering hypocrites in Washington.

As I lie dead, please grant my last request. Help me inform the American people, the silent majority who have not yet voiced their opinions."

In 1967, 'Vietnam Veterans Against the War' was formed. They demonstrated all over America. Many of them were in wheelchairs or on crutches. People watched on television as Vietnam 'heroes' threw away the medals they had won fighting in the war. One shouted: "Here's my merit badges for murder." Another apologised to the Vietnamese people and claimed that : "I hope that someday I can return to Vietnam and help to rebuild that country we tore apart."

The Mass Media and the War

The US administration, unlike most governments at war, made no official attempt to censure the reporting in the Vietnam War. Every night on colour television people saw pictures of dead and wounded marines. Dean Rusk, US Secretary of State, pointed out that: "This was the first struggle fought on television in everybody's living room every day... whether ordinary people can sustain a war effort under that kind of daily hammering is a very large question."

Newspaper reporters and television commentators were free to question the wisdom of fighting the war. Military leaders accused their critics of being "unpatriotic" and guilty of "helping the enemy." The Generals were especially angered by the way the media covered the Tet offensive. General Maxwell Taylor wrote later: "The picture of a few flaming Saigon houses, presented by a gloomy-voiced telecaster as an instance of the destruction caused in the capital, created the inevitable impression that this was the way it was in all or most of Saigon."

Admiral Grant Sharp was another critic of the mass media. He argued: "The reality of the 1968 Tet offensive was that Hanoi had taken a big gamble and had lost on the battlefield, but they won a solid psychological victory in the United States." Sharp believed that the biased reporting of the Tet offensive convinced the American public and the government that the war was being lost and the only option was to withdraw from Vietnam.

One of the most influential acts during the war was the decision of 'Life' to fill one edition of its magazine with photographs of the 242 US soldiers killed in Vietnam during one week of the fighting.

It was this type of reporting that encouraged General Westmoreland, commander of US troops in Vietnam, to accuse the mass media of helping to bring about a NLF victory. However, defenders of the mass media claimed that reporters were only reflecting the changing opinions of the American people towards the war.

Public opinion polls carried out at the time suggest that the tax increases to pay for the war and the death of someone they knew, were far more influential than the mass media in changing people's attitude towards the war.

Vietnamization

In March, 1968, Lyndon Johnson announced that he would not stand for re-election in the forthcoming presidential election. The Vietnam War was a central issue in the campaign, with both Hubert Humphrey, the Democratic candidate, and Richard Nixon, his Republican opponent, promising to end the war by obtaining an "honourable peace". Humphrey, who had been Johnson's Vice-President and had been closely associated with the failures of the previous four years, was beaten by Nixon in the election.

Soon after taking office, President Nixon introduced his policy of "vietnamization". The plan was to encourage the South Vietnamese to take more responsibility for fighting the war. It was hoped that this policy would eventually enable the United States to withdraw gradually all their soldiers from Vietnam.

To increase the size of the ARVN, a mobilisation law was passed that called up into the army all men in South Vietnam aged between seventeen and forty-three.

In June, 1969, Nixon announced the first of the US troop withdrawals. The 540,000 US troops were to be reduced by 25,000. Another 60,000 were to leave the following December.

Nixon's advisers told him that they feared that the gradual removal of all US troops would eventually result in a NLF victory.

'Civilian Self-Defense' unit in North Vietnam

It was therefore agreed that the only way that America could avoid a humiliating defeat was to negotiate a peace agreement in the talks that were taking place in Paris. In an effort to put pressure on North Vietnam in these talks, Nixon developed what has become known as the 'Madman Theory'. Bob Haldeman, one of the US chief negotiators, was told to give the impression that President Nixon was mentally unstable and that his hatred of communism was so fanatical that if the war continued for much longer he was liable to resort to nuclear weapons against North Vietnam.

Another Nixon innovation was the secret 'Phoenix Program'. Vietnamese were trained by the CIA to infiltrate peasant communities and discover the names of NLF sympathisers. When they had been identified, "Death Squads" were sent in to execute them. Between 1968 and 1971, an estimated 40,974 members of of the NLF were killed in this way. It was hoped that the "Phoenix Program" would result in the destruction of the NLF organisation, but, as on previous occasions, the NLF was able to replace its losses by recruiting from the local population and by arranging for volunteers to be sent from North Vietnam.

Cambodia and Laos

Since the beginning of the Vietnam War, the NLF had used bases situated just inside the borders of neighbouring Cambodia. For many years US military advisers had wanted these bases to be bombed. President Johnson had rejected this strategy as he feared it would undermine the anti-communist government of Prince Sihanouk.

Soon after becoming president, Richard Nixon gave permission for the bombing of Cambodia. In an effort to avoid international protest at this action, it was decided to keep information about these bombing raids hidden. Pilots were sworn to secrecy and their 'operational logs' were falsified.

The bombing failed to destroy the NLF bases and so in April, 1970, Nixon decided to send in troops to finish off the job. The invasion of Cambodia provoked a wave of demonstrations in the United States and in one of these, four students were killed when National guardsmen opened fire at Kent State University. In the days that followed, 450 colleges closed in protest against the killings.

The arrival of US marines in Cambodia also created hostility amongst the local population. The Cambodian communist movement, the Khmer Rouge, had received little support from the peasants before the United States invasion. Now they were in a position to appeal to their nationalist sentiments and claimed that Cambodia was about to be taken over by the United States. During 1970 and 1971, membership of the Khmer Rouge grew rapidly.

Laos, another country bordering Vietnam, was also invaded by US troops. As with Cambodia, this action increased the support for the communists (Pathet Lao) and by 1973, they controlled most of the country.

My Lai

In 1971, Colonel Robert Heinl reported that: "By every conceivable indicator, our army that now remains in Vietnam is in a state approaching collapse with individual units avoiding or having refused combat, murdering their officers and non-commissioned officers, drug-ridden and dispirited where not near-mutinous."

For sometime stories had been circulating about deteriorating behaviour amongst US soldiers. Efforts were made by the US army to suppress information about the raping and killing of Vietnamese

John Filo shot dead at Kent State University

civilians but eventually, after considerable pressure from certain newspapers, it was decided to put Lieutenant William Calley on trial for war-crimes. In March, 1971, Calley was found guilty of murdering 109 Vietnamese civilians at My Lai. He was sentenced to life imprisonment but he only served three years before being released from prison.

During the war, twenty-five US soldiers were charged with war-crimes but William Calley was the only one found guilty. Calley received considerable sympathy from the American public when he stated: "When my troops were getting massacred and mauled by an enemy I couldn't see, I couldn't feel, I couldn't touch... nobody in the military system ever described them anything other than Communists." Even Seymour Hersh, the reporter who had first published details of the My Lai killings, admitted that Calley was "as much a victim as the people he shot."

Critics of the war argued that as the US government totally disregarded the welfare of Vietnamese civilians when it ordered the use of weapons such as napalm and agent orange, it was hypocritical to charge individual soldiers with war-crimes. As the mother of one of the soldiers accused of killing civilians at My Lai asserted: "I sent them (the US army) a good boy, and they made him a murderer."

Philip Caputo, another US marine accused of killing innocent civilians, wrote later that it was the nature of the war that resulted in so many war-crimes being committed: "In a guerrilla war, the line between legitimate and illegitimate killing is blurred. The policies of free-fire zones, in which a soldier is permitted to shoot at any human target, armed or unarmed... further confuse the fighting man's moral senses."

The publicity surrounding the My Lai massacre proved to be an important turning point in American public opinion. It illustrated the deterioration that was taking place in the behaviour of the US troops and undermined the moral argument about the need to save Vietnam from the "evils of communism". Vietnam was not only being destroyed in order to "save it" but it was becoming clear that those responsible for defeating communism were being severely damaged by their experiences.

A Negotiated Peace

Peace talks between representatives from United States, South Vietnam, North Vietnam and the NLF had been taking place in Paris since January, 1969. By 1972, Nixon, like Johnson before him, had been gradually convinced that a victory in Vietnam was unobtainable.

In October, 1972, the negotiators came close to agreeing to a formula to end the war. The plan was that US troops would withdraw from Vietnam in exchange for a cease-fire and the return of 566 American prisoners held in Hanoi. It was also agreed that the governments in North and South Vietnam would remain in power until new elections could be arranged to unite the whole country.

The main problem with this formula was that whereas the US troops would leave the country, the North Vietnamese troops could remain in their positions in the south. In an effort to put pressure on North Vietnam to withdraw its troops, President Nixon ordered a new series of air-raids on Hanoi and Haiphong. It was the most intense bombing attack in world history. In eleven days, 100,000 bombs were dropped on the two cities. The destructive power was equivalent to five times that of the atom bomb used on Hiroshima. This bombing campaign was condemned throughout the world. Newspaper headlines included: "Genocide", "Stone-Age Barbarism" and "Savage and Senseless".

The North Vietnamese refused to change the terms of the

Air-raid shelters in Hanoi.

agreement and so in January, 1973, Nixon agreed to sign the peace plan that had been proposed in October. However, the bombing had proved to be popular with many of the American public as they had the impression that North Vietnam had been "bombed into submission."

The End of the War

The last US combat troops left in March, 1973. It was an uneasy peace and by 1974, serious fighting had broken out between the NLF and the AVRN. Although the US continued to supply the South Vietnamese government with military equipment, their army had great difficulty using it effectively.

President Thieu of South Vietnam appealed to President Nixon for more financial aid. Nixon was sympathetic but the United States Congress was not and the move was blocked. At its peak US aid to South Vietnam had reached 30 billion dollars a year. By 1974 it had fallen to 1 billion. Starved of funds, Thieu had difficulty paying the wages of his large army and desertion became a major problem.

The spring of 1975 saw a series of NLF victories. After important areas such as Danang and Hue were lost in March, panic swept through the AVRN. Senior officers, fearing what would happen after the establishment of an NLF government, abandoned

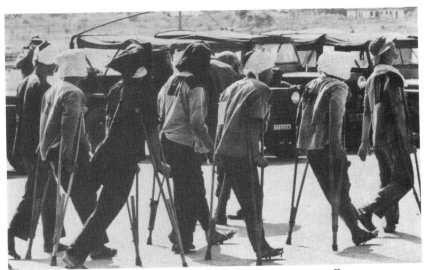

NLF soldiers released after the cease-fire.

their men and went into hiding.

President Thieu announced in desperation that he had a signed letter from Richard Nixon promising military help if it appeared that the NLF were winning in South Vietnam. However, Nixon was no longer in a position to fulfil his promise as he had been forced to resign over Watergate. The new president, Gerald Ford, a strong supporter of US involvement in Vietnam, tried to raise support for the South Vietnamese government but the Senate was adamant that as far as it was concerned, the war was over.

On April 23, 1975, President Ford told the American people: "Today Americans can regain the sense of pride that existed before Vietnam. But it cannot be achieved by refighting a war that is finished." Two days later, President Thieu, accusing the United States of betrayal, resigned and left the country. He was quickly followed by other South Vietnamese leaders and the remaining American advisers.

The NLF arrived in Saigon on April 30, 1975. After declaring that Vietnam was now a united country, Saigon was renamed Ho Chi Minh City.

1975 also saw the setting up of communist governments in Laos and Cambodia. These victories had been at a terrible cost to the people of these countries. Between 1961 and 1975 an estimated 10% of the people living in Vietnam, Cambodia and Laos had died. In the same period, 56,869 US troops were killed and another 153,329 were seriously wounded. The long-term psychological damage to the three million soldiers who fought in Vietnam and the resulting social problems are still being counted.

43

The Effect of the War on Vietnam and the United States

(1) W.E. Garrett has been a reporter in South-East Asia for twenty-five years. He currently works for the magazine, 'National Geographic'
Ten years ago... the victorious North Vietnamese Army poured into Saigon. In the decade since, a million Vietnamese and ethnic Chinese had fled afoot and by boat. Some 15,000 children fathered by American GIs have endured a decade of torment and rejection. As many as 10,000 of our former allies - considered criminals by the present government - remain in prison.

(2) Nguyen Thi Anh was a member of the National Liberation Front. In this passage she explains what happened to her when she was captured by the South Vietnamese army.
They tried to force me to confess that I was a member of the Vietcong. I refused to make such a statement and so they stuck needles under the tips of my ten fingers saying that if I did not write down what they wanted and admit to being a member of the Vietcong, they would continue to torture me. I was determined to say nothing. I was extremely angry at the enemy and I loved my country so much. This was because every day bombs and shells were falling and the blood and the bones of my people appeared before my eyes... I was extremely outraged and would never come out with any information. They tied my nipples to an electric wire and they gave me electric shocks, knocking me to the floor every time that they did so. They said that if they did not get the necessary information they would continue with the torture. Two American advisers were always standing on either side of me.

(3) In 1967, the journalist Martha Gellhorn visited Vietnam. Her reports were published in the 'Ladies' Home Journal'.
In the children's ward of the Qui Nhon province hospital I saw for the first time what Napalm does. A child of seven, the size of our four-year-olds, lay in the cot by the door. Napalm had burned his face and back and one hand. The burned skin looked like swollen red meat; the fingers on his hand were stretched out, burned rigid. A scrap of cheesecloth covered him, for weight is intolerable, but so too is air.

(4) A housewife from New Jersey, the mother of six, decided to go to Vietnam and adopt three Vietnamese children. While she was there she visited several hospitals.

I had heard and read that napalm melts the flesh, and I thought that's nonsense, because I can put a roast in the oven and the fat will melt but the meat stays there. Well, I went and saw these children burned by napalm, and it's absolutely true. The chemical reaction of this napalm does melt the flesh, and the flesh runs right down their faces onto their chests and it sits there and grows there... These children can't turn their heads, they were so thick with flesh... And when gangrene sets in, they cut off their hands or fingers or their feet.

(5) Richard West was In Vietnam after U.S. combat troops left the country in 1973. Here he describes some of the problems that existed in Saigon before the NLF victory in 1975.

A few days ago I heard a girl weeping because her sister, a prostitute, had died of VD at the age of 19. She was one of the hundreds of thousands of drug addicts in Saigon who have grown still more desperate since the heroin ran out and who have to find £4 or £5 a day to 'shoot up' boiled opium seed or sleeping pills... one sees countless young people, army deserters and crippled veterans wearing injection scabs on their wrists or ankles; the limbless 'shoot up' through a vein at the side of the head... the epidemics of VD and drugs are largely attributable not to the Saigon regime but to the Americans who departed two years ago, leaving their grisly souvenirs.

(6) Joseph Buttinger is an American writer who has attempted to document the effect that the war had on the people of Vietnam.

The total tonnage of bombs dropped between 1964 and the end of 1971 was 6.2 million. This means that the U.S. has dropped 300 pounds of bombs for every man, woman, and child in Indochina, and 22 tons of bombs for every square mile. Enormous craters dot the landscape in many regions covering dozens of square miles. Hundreds of villages were totally destroyed by bombs and napalm, forests over vast areas defoliated, making the land infertile for years, and crops destroyed, with little or no consideration for the needs of the people, merely on suspicion that some of the crop might benefit the enemy... The total number of people made refugees is more than 5 million... The rise of the refugee population in South Vietnam was partly due also to the past American policy of removing from countless villages, for strategic reasons, the entire population, and of putting these unfortunate people in what were called refugee camps or relocation centres.

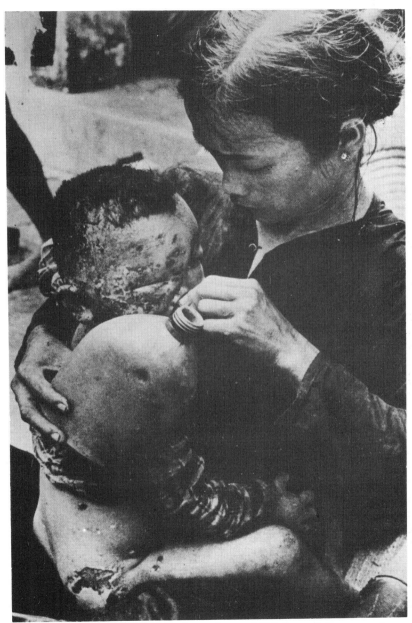

Vietnamese mother comforts her child burnt by napalm.

(7) In 1982 four war veterans returned to Vietnam. This group included Bob Muller, a former lieutenant in the Marines who is paralysed from the waist down after being shot through the spine in Vietnam in 1969. When they returned home they called for the United States government to pay compensation to the Vietnamese people.

In Ho Chi Minh City we visited two hospitals which house the deformed children thought to be victims of Agent Orange. Since the dumping on Vietnam of some 11 million gallons of Agent Orange there has been a huge increase in the frequency of genetic malfunctions. Children have been born without eyes, with twisted, mangled limbs, even without brains. In the main hospital in Tay Ninh, a quarter of all births are miscarriages... Hydrocephalus, or water on the brain, is thought to be one of the many malformations attributable to Agent Orange. At the Tu Do Hospital, doctors need to perform some 100 operations a year on hydrocephalic babies. The operation required is a relatively simple one, frequently performed in the West, using a special silicone tube. But the Vietnamese doctors cannot carry out the operations because they have no silicone tubes... The tubes are manufactured in the US and America has imposed a complete embargo on exports to Vietnam.

Vietnamese children deformed by Agent Orange

(8) John Kerry, a naval officer who was awarded several medals for his efforts in Vietnam became active in the 'Vietnam Veterans Against the War' organisation in the late 1960s. In 1984 he was elected to the US Senate.

Several months ago in Detroit we had an investigation at which over 150 honorably discharged, and many very highly decorated, veterans testified to war crimes committed in South-East Asia. These were not isolated incidents but crimes committed on a day to day basis with a full awareness of officers at all levels of command.

They told stories that at times they had personally raped, cut-off ears, cut-off heads, taped wires from portable telephones to human genitals and turned up the power, cut-off limbs, blown up bodies, randomly shot at civilians, razed villages in a fashion reminiscent of Genghis Khan, shot cattle and dogs for fun, poisoned food stocks, and generally ravaged the countryside of South Vietnam...

I would like to talk to you a little bit about what the result is of the feelings these men carry with them after coming back from Vietnam. The country doesn't know it yet but it has created a monster, a monster in the form of millions of men who have been taught to deal and trade in violence.

(9) Stanley Karnov first visited Vietnam as a reporter for 'Time' magazine in 1959. He has written several books on South-East Asia and is acknowledged as having a deep understanding of the subject. While researching the film series, 'Vietnam: A Television History', he interviewed many American soldiers who took part in the war.

The use of drugs was so widespread that, according to an official estimate made in 1971, nearly one third of the troops were addicted to opium or heroin, and marijuana smoking had become routine.

The average age of the American soldier in Vietnam was nineteen, seven years younger than his father had been in World War II, which made him more vulnerable to the psychological strains of the struggle - strains that were aggravated by the special tension of Vietnam, where every peasant might be a Vietcong terrorist.

A Veterans Administration psychiatrist, Dr. Jack Ewart, estimates that some seven hundred thousand veterans suffer from various forms of "post-traumatic stress disorder," the modern term for "shell shock" in World War 1 and "battle fatigue" in World War II. Vietnam caused many more cases than those conflicts, however. Its symptoms, which can occur ten or fifteen years later, range from panic and rage to anxiety, depression, and emotional paralysis. Crime, suicide, alcoholism, narcotics addiction, divorce, and unemployment among Vietnam veterans far outstrip the norm.

(10) Thomas Powers was a reporter for the United Press International Agency. Between 1964 and 1968 he covered the activities of both Anti-Vietnam and Civil Rights Movements.

The Harlem riot in the summer of 1964 had been followed a year later by the far larger and more serious uprising in the Watts section of Los Angeles. Serious disturbances occurred in several midwestern cities in the summer of 1966, but nothing had prepared the country for the size and violence of the urban riots which began in Newark on Thursday, July 13, and in Detroit ten days later.

During the five days of rioting in Newark, 26 people were killed, 1,200 were injured, and 1,300 were arrested. More than $10 million worth of damage was reported... Overcrowded schools, decrepit housing, hospitals with beds in the hallways, a lack of jobs all made Newark a classic example of what would soon be called a crisis of the cities... Part of the bitter, reckless mood was the failure of Johnson's war on poverty, the readiest explanation of which was the cost of the war in Vietnam.

(11) Steve volunteered for the US army at 16. After serving two terms in Vietnam he suffered a mental breakdown. While recuperating at home he had a fit and in the process nearly murdered his mother. Since then he has lived on his own in a tent in the forests of the Washington Olympic Peninsula. It has been estimated that over a thousand Vietnam Veterans unable to adapt to normal society live like this in these remote forests.

I went through an army training course. On this course were Japanese and Chinese American military wearing communist uniforms with red stars and carrying communist built weapons. They would capture you and they beat you, took your clothes off and hit you with rifle butts... They hung me up with my wrists for over an hour. Then they cut me down and tied my hands behind my back... Three men came in - you have to remember that this was after a week of going without food, you've been beat up ten or fifteen times, you've had no sleep and they have been constantly hammering at you trying to find out where your unit's at. These three men brought out guns and fired blanks at me. Only at the time I did not know they were blanks... being forced to stand in certain positions, being kicked, slapped, questioned the whole time, having to crawl through garbage and human faeces... Chinese music and North Vietnam music being played all the time. Ho Chi Minh's speeches would come on. So by the time I finished four of these camps... When I got to go into action. When I went to Vietnam. The only thing that was going through my mind was exactly what was planned. That was to kill communists. I became a machine. A very effective machine. I was very good at what I did. I survived.

There was a point when I think I enjoyed killing. I came through that. Then there was a time when I did not want to kill anything again... I cracked under pressure after twenty-two months. They put me in a straight jacket. They kept me doped up and after twenty-four hours I was back in the United States.

Part of it is the guilt. It's having to leave wounded comrades which had nothing to do with what I grew up with. John Wayne, Audie Murphy, none of them left their comrades. They all got medals... They never left comrades to be hacked up into small pieces.

I would like to live a productive life. I would like to go to sleep at night without waking up in a cold sweat. I would like to have a loving relationship that does not involve fear, that does not involve all the things that has been a gift from the government. They failed to turn me back to the person I used to be. They failed to turn me back to the guy from down the block.

(12) Tim O'Brien served in the Vietnam War as an infantryman. Here he describes the dangers of going out on patrol. Over 10,000 US soldiers lost limbs during the Vietnam war, a considerable number of these injuries were caused by NLF mines.

The most feared mine was the "Bouncing Betty'. It was conical shaped, three prongs jutting out of the soil. When your foot hit the prong, a charge went off that shot the mine into the air, a yard high, showering shrapnel everywhere. It's a mine that goes after the lower torso: a terrible mine... On one occasion after my company had encamped and sent out patrols there was a large explosion only 200 yards away... We raced out there and only two men were living out of a patrol of eight or so. Just a mess. It was like a stew, full of meat and flesh and red tissue and white bone.

(13) Gloria Emerson tells the story of John Young who was ambushed by the NLF when leading a patrol in 1968.

Young was trying to get to a clump of trees when he was hit twice by an AK-47 rifle... He was still lying on his stomach in the gully when he felt the bayonets in his back. It was about nine o'clock in the morning. He had not even noticed how much he was bleeding or the pieces of bone that had been pushed through his skin and were sticking out of his leg like huge toothpicks... North Vietnamese officers interrogated him. He would tell them nothing except his name, rank, serial number, date of birth. They yanked his leg and hit him with the butt of a weapon on the head and in the back. He does not think he screamed when the Vietnamese twisted and bent his shattered leg. He hated them too much, Young said, to do that, so he stayed silent and let the pain shine.

(14) Colonel Robinson Risner spent seven and a half years in a prison in Hanoi. He was one of the 600 members of the US airforce who was shot down and captured by the North Vietnamese. Colonel Risner was released from captivity after the cease-fire agreement in 1973.

When I got out of my plane I found myself looking right down a gun bore... I had to make a decision. Was I going to make a fight of it. I already had a gun aimed right at my head. And I changed my mind. I remember telling the guys that I would never be captured but I changed my mind...

My wrists and arms were tied behind my back. The two arms were close together which pulled my shoulders out of joint. They did some similar things to my legs... During the night I heard someone screaming in the distance. I thought they were torturing another prisoner. And I felt so sorry for him. And then I came more closely to consciousness and found out it was me. I was the one who was doing the screaming. They tortured me all night and by daylight they had reduced me to such a state I gave them more than my name, rank and date of birth... I tried to endure the pain knowing that an American military man should endure torture until he dies. I tried my best but my best was not good enough... I found I was not as strong as I thought I was. I found I could not be tortured to death. My will would give before my heart stopped beating. It was very disconcerting. I lived in abject misery for the rest of the time I was a prisoner in Vietnam.

Vietnamese shelter from US bombing raid.

(15) Bruce joined the US navy at seventeen. He was trained for secret undercover work in Vietnam. He now lives on his own in a house in the forests of the Washington Olympic Peninsula.

I had to destroy villages, kill everybody there and then leave communist arms there. I realised what we were doing. It made sense then... You don't take a person's life and not have guilt feelings about it. Anyone who says they can and not feel guilty about it is lying.

One chap got a chest wound. we had to go into the bush. The Vietcong were there. The chap with the chest wound was making a hell of a noise. I did away with him myself. I had to to save me and the other fellow... I did not want to die... Every means that I had to survive I used. The gun played a real big part in that. A man with a gun can do anything. Anything. Its the awesome power that you have in your hands. It's a real feeling of power. I love it. These guns are my life, they really are.

When I first got back I spent time in the penitentiary in California. I killed a man right here in the United States... I do not trust anyone now. I would rather trust a dog than a person. A person is a vicious animal. I'm not normal by any means. A normal person can handle society. I can't. I do not like people... I'll be pleased when its done. When death comes I think I'll welcome it.

(16) Jeff Needle was a Vietnam Veteran who protested against the war when he returned to the United States. He wrote and distributed a booklet called 'Please Read This'.

A very sad thing happened while we were there - to everyone. It happened slowly and gradually so no one noticed when it happened. We began slowly with each death and every casualty until there were so many deaths and so many wounded, we started to treat death and loss of limbs with callousness, and it happens because the human mind can't hold that much suffering and survive.

(17) After the Vietnam War was over some American soldiers admitted acts of atrocities against the Vietnamese people. Here a former American intelligence officer describes what happened to people suspected of being members of the NLF.

I never knew an individual to be detained as a VC suspect who ever lived through an interrogation... and that included quite a number of individuals... They all died. There was never any reasonable establishment of the fact that any of those individuals was, in fact, cooperating with the Vietcong, but they all died and the majority were either tortured to death or things like thrown from helicopters.

(18) In villages where the population was suspected of helping the NLF, torture and executions of civilians sometimes took place. On 16 March, 1968, American troops killed more than 500 people from the village of My Lai. A young helicopter gunner, Ronald Ridenhour who saw the massacre wrote to President Nixon about the incident. Attempts by the army to cover-up what had taken place were undermined by the journalist, Seymour Hersh, who managed to persuade several soldiers involved in the massacre to talk about what taken place at My Lai.

Some of Calley's men thought it was breakfast time as they walked in; a few families were gathered in front of their homes cooking rice over a small fire. Without a direct order, the first platoon also began rounding up the villagers... Sledge remembered thinking that "if there were VC around, they had plenty of time to leave before we came in. We didn't tiptoe in there."

The killings began without warning... Stanley saw "some old women and some little children - fifteen or twenty of them - in a group around a temple where some incense was burning. They were kneeling and crying and praying, and various soldiers... walked by and executed these women and children by shooting them in the head with their rifles.

There were few physical protests from the people; about eighty of them were taken quietly from their homes and herded together in the

It says: "Sorry, but programming omitted factor of human spirit."

plaza area. A few hollered out, "No VC, No VC,"... Women were huddled against children, vainly trying to save them. Some continued to chant, "No VC." Others simply said, "No. No. No."

Carter recalled that some GIs were shouting and yelling during the massacre: "The boys enjoyed it. When someone laughs and jokes about what they're doing, they have to be enjoying it." A GI said, "Hey, I got me another one." Another said, "Chalk up one for me." Even Captain Medina was having a good time, Carter thought: "You can tell when someone enjoys their work." Few members of Charlie Company protested that day. For the most part, those who didn't like what was going on kept their thoughts to themselves.

By nightful the Viet Cong were back in My Lai, helping the survivors bury the dead. It took five days. Most of the funeral speeches were made by the Communist guerrillas. Nguyen Bat was not a communist at the time of the massacre, but the incident changed his mind. "After the. shooting," he said, "all the villagers became Communists."

(19) Philip Caputo volunteered for the US Marines after hearing a speech by President Kennedy on the dangers of communism. After serving a year in Vietnam he was court-martialled for the murder of two Vietnamese civilians. He was found not guilty but received a reprimand for making false statements to his senior officers. In his book, "A Rumour of War', Caputo attempts to explain how the Vietnam War turned some US soldiers into people who could commit atrocities.

The war was mostly a matter of enduring weeks of expectant waiting and, at random intervals, of conducting vicious manhunts through jungles and swamps where snipers harassed us constantly and booby traps cut us down one by one... At times, the comradeship that was the war's only redeeeming quality caused some of the worst crimes - acts of retribution for friends who had been killed. Some men could not withstand the stress of guerrilla-fighting: the hair-trigger alertness constantly demanded of them, the feeling that the enemy was everywhere, the inability to distinguish civilians from combatants created emotional pressures which built to such a point that a trivial provocation could make these men explode and the blind destructiveness of a mortar shell... I felt sorry for those children, (soldiers arriving in Vietnam for the first time) knowing that they would all grow old in the land of endless dying. I pitied them, knowing that out of every ten, one would die, two would be maimed for life, another two would be less seriously wounded and sent out to fight again, and all the rest would be wounded in other, more hidden ways.

(20) Colonel R. Heinl spent 27 years in the Marines and has written several books on military matters. In the early 70s he investigated the morale of the armed forces involved in the Vietnam War.

The morale, discipline and battleworthiness of the U.S. Armed Forces are, with a few salient exceptions, lower and worse than at any time in this century and possibly in the history of the United States... In 1970, the Army had 65,643 deserters, or roughly the equivalent of four infantry divisions. This desertion rate (52.3 soldiers per thousand) is well over twice the peak-rate for Korea (22.5 per thousand).

"Frag incidents" or just "fragging" is current soldier slang in Vietnam for the murder or attempted murder of strict, unpopular, or just aggressive officers and NCOs... the Pentagon has now disclosed that fraggings in 1970 (209) have more than doubled those of the previous year (96)...Bounties, raised by common subscription in amounts running anywhere from $50 to $1,000, have been widely reported put on the heads of leaders whom the privates and Sp4s want to rub out.

In 1966, the Navy discharged 170 drug offenders. Three years later (1969), 3,800 were discharged. Last year in 1970, the total jumped to over 5,000... In April, for example, members of a Congressional investigating subcommittee reported that 10 to 15% of our troops in Vietnam are now using high-grade heroin, and that drug addiction there is "of epidemic proportions."

(21) The popularity of films like 'Uncommon Valor', 'Missing in Action' and 'Rambo' have helped support the idea that there are many soldiers still in Vietnamese prisons. Here Marvin Gentleman, a Professor of American history, puts forward arguments against this view.

Although only 1,830 Americans are still listed as missing in action in Vietnam, plus 560 in Laos and 100 in Cambodia - a far smaller percentage than after the Civil War, World War I, or World War II - heavily financed campaigns, aided by the government, seek to exploit the emotions of their loved ones by promulgating the preposterous myth, contrary to all evidence and common sense, that the Vietnamese and Laotians are still holding many of these men as prisoners... Meanwhile, there are indeed many tens of thousands of imprisoned Vietnam veterans, but these are not the subject of popular entertainment and jingoist propaganda. In 1978, the Government Accounting Office estimated that there were then 125,000 Vietnam veterans (over twice the total of those reported killed) not in Laotian or Vietnamese but in American prisons.

(22) Micheal Parris is a film critic who has made a detailed study of how the cinema has dealt with the Vietnam War.

The American film industry can hardly be accused of ignoring the Vietnam War. But what it has ignored are some of the more unpleasant aspects of that conflict. No film has yet presented any real justification for Americans going to South-East Asia other than in the most vague terms such as to combat 'treaty obligations'. No American feature has dealt with the end of the war, the withdrawal of American troops in 1973 or the subsequent fall of Saigon in 1975. It appears that Americans have yet to come to terms with defeat and it seems fashionable to soften the truth with phrases like 'the war that nobody won'... All of which diverts attention from the harsh reality - that America suffered a costly military defeat. Other aspects of the war have also been ignored in the cinema's view of events. There has been no mention of the de-foliation programmes or reference to other chemical weapons; nor of the massive bombing campaigns against North Vietnam or Laos.

The most recent features have dealt with commando raids into present-day Vietnam to release prisoners-of-war still held by the communists. *Uncommon Valor* (1983), *Missing in Action* (1984) and the phenomenally successful *Rambo* have all shown that the communists can be beaten and have attempted to restore military self-respect.

Poster for Hollywood film on the Vietnam War

(23) Joel Swerdlow is a newspaper reporter who co-wrote 'To Heal a Nation', a book about the building of the 'Vietnam Veterans' Memorial' in Washington. The memorial contains the names of the 58,000 who died in the Vietnam War or are still missing.

With more than 150,000 people in town for the dedication, Washington's hotels, restaurants, and streets filled with vets. It was, said one happy ex-GI, "one helluva party." After many beers, a veteran said he had won the Medal of Honour but was afraid of how people would react. To the cheers of a crowded bar, he opened his suitcase, took out the medal with its blue ribbon, and put it on for the first time.

A man in a wheelchair slowly pushed through another bar that was filled to capacity. At first no one noticed him. Slowly, the noise faded, and then people reached out to touch him.

A former medic sat in a corner, crying. He pushed away all who tried to console him. "I should have saved more, " he kept saying. "I should have saved more."

On Saturday, November 13, Vietnam veterans marched down Constitution Avenue to the memorial in one of the largest processions the nation's capital had seen since John F. Kennedy's funeral.

Following speeches by dignitaries, the crowd sang "God Bless America," and paused for a moment of silence. "Ladies and gentlemen," Jan Scruggs said, "the Vietnam Veterans Memorial is now dedicated."

The tightly packed mass surged forward, crushing fences erected for crowd control. As thousands of hands strained to touch names, a lone GI climbed to the top of the wall, put a bugle to his lips and played.

All afternoon, all night, the next day and the next and the next for an unbroken stream of months and years, millions of Americans have come and experienced that frozen moment.

The names have a power, a life, all of their own. Even on the coldest days, sunlight makes them warm to the touch... Perhaps by touching, people renew their faith in love and in life, or perhaps they better understand sacrifice and sorrow.

"We're with you," they say. "We will never forget."

The 'Vietnam Veterans' Memorial' in Washington.

Work Section

Important figures in the Vietnam Conflict

Match the names in the first column with the facts in the second column.

1	Ho Chi Minh	(a) assassinated in South Vietnam in 1963
2	Vo Nguyen Giap	(b) Buddhist monk who committed suicide
3	Dwight Eisenhower	(c) leader of the Chinese communists
4	Ngo Dinh Diem	(d) Commander of US forces, 1964-68
5	Thich Quang Duc	(e) President of the USA, 1952-1960
6	Lyndon Johnson	(f) started withdrawing US troops in 1969
7	Mao Zedong	(g) imprisoned for the My Lai massacre
8	W. Westmoreland	(h) first president of North Vietnam
9	Richard Nixon	(i) fled to Taiwan in 1975
10	William Calley	(j) introduced 'Strategic Hamlet' theory in 1962
11	Nguyen Thieu	(k) planned the Vietminh attack on Dien Bien Phu
12	John Kennedy	(l) ordered bombing of North Vietnam in 1964

Key Points

Write out a brief explanation of the following key aspects of the Vietnam War. Page references are given after each word.

1 Buddhism (6, 18-19)
2 Vietminh (7-10)
3 Dien Bien Phu (9-10)
4 Geneva Conference (10-12)
5 ARVN (12, 25, 37, 42)
6 NLF (14-16, 24-27, 39, 43)
7 Domino Theory (16, 20)
8 Strategic Hamlet (17-18)
9 Operation 34A (21)
10 Gulf of Tonkin (21-22)

11 Operation Rolling Thunder (22)
12 Guerrilla Warfare (23-27)
13 Search and Destroy (27)
14 Ho Chi Minh Trail (17-28)
15 Napalm (28, 45-46)
16 Operation Ranch Hand (30, 48)
17 Tet Offensive (32-33)
18 Vietnamization (37)
19 Phoenix Program (38)
20 My Lai (39-41, 54-55)

GCSE Coursework Assessment

You are a member of a Senate Investigation into the consequences of the Vietnam War. After reading through the testimonies of the witnesses on pages 45-58: (a) make a list of the affects of the war on Vietnam and the United States and (b) explain how these problems could be solved.

Outline Essay

John King Fairbanks has written that the main cause of the American failure in Vietnam was: "the profound American cultural ignorance of Vietnamese history, values, problems, and motives." Explain what he means by this statement (page references in parenthesis).

History

Vietnam involved in long struggle to obtain its freedom from China (5), Japan (7-8) and France (5-6, 8-10) before the arrival of the United States.

Two important points arise out of this:
1 Main motivation of Vietnamese guerrillas was to obtain independence.
2. Vietnamese were willing to fight a long-term war. This was not true of the USA.

Values

Majority of Vietnamese people were Buddhists (18-19).
Catholicism was closely identified with French Colonialism (6, 18).
Diem ruled a Catholic dominated administration (13-14, 18).
Policies such as 'Strategic Hamlet' programme, were in conflict with traditional Buddhist beliefs (17-18).

Problems

The main concern of the Vietnamese peasants was land reform.
50% of the land owned by 2% of the population (25).
Catholic Church largest land-owner in Vietnam (18).

South Vietnamese government and USA associated with large land-owners whereas NLF introduced land reform in areas they controlled (15-16).

Motives

NLF was a combination of different groups that were hostile to military rule, catholics, western controlled administrations and large landowners (15).

Independence rather than a desire for communism was the main objective of NLF.

US tactics: Heavy bombing (22, 28, 30, 48); strategic hamlet programme (17-18); search and destroy (27); retaliation against guerrilla warfare (25-27, 49, 54-55) increased resistance and encouraged support for the NLF.

Statements

Explain whether you agree with the following statements. Use information from the text and the sources to support your arguments (page references in parenthesis).

The CIA made the defeat of the NLF more difficult after helping to remove President Diem. (12-14, 18-20)

The NLF was more a nationalist than a communist organisation. (6-8, 14-16, 24-26)

The events in South-East Asia between 1965-75 support the idea of the 'Domino Theory'. (16, 20, 39, 42-43)

One of the major reasons why the NLF gained control of South Vietnam was that the United States failed to gain the support of the Buddhist population. (5-6, 18-20)

Heavy bombing of North Vietnam was both immoral and a military failure. (21-23, 28-30, 41, 45-48)

Guerrilla warfare is a tactic used by cowards. (23-27, 51)

The Tet Offensive was a victory for the NLF. (32-33)

The United States peace movement and the mass media helped the NLF gain control of South Vietnam. (33-37)

Vietnamization would have been successful if it had been used five years earlier. (12-13, 16-18, 37-38)

Bibliography

Bator, V.	*Vietnam: A Diplomatic Tragedy*	Faber & Faber, 1967
Burchett, W.	*Inside Story of the Guerrilla War*	I.P., 1954
Buttinger, J.	*Vietnam: A Political History*	Andre Deutsch, 1969
Buttinger, J.	*A Dragon Defiant*	David & Charles, 1972
Cameron, J.	*Witness*	Gollancz, 1966
Caputo, P.	*A Rumour of War*	Macmillan, 1977
Coates, K. (ed.)	*Prevent the Crime of Silence*	Allen Lane, 1971
Cooper, C.	*The Lost Crusade*	MacGibbon & Kee, 1971
Draper, T.	*Abuse of Power*	Penguin, 1969
Emerson, G.	*Winners and Losers*	Random House, 1975
Fall, B.	*Vietnam Witness*	Pall Mall, 1966
FitzGerald, F.	*Fire in the Lake*	Macmillan, 1972
Halberstam, D	*Ho Chi Minh*	Barrie & Jackson, 1971
Gerassi, J.	*North Vietnam: A Documentary*	Allen & Unwin, 147
Gentleman, M.(ed.)	*Vietnam: Documents & Opinions*	Penguin, 1966
Gentleman, M.(ed.)	*Vietnam and America*	Grove Press, 1985
Greene, F.	*Vietnam! Vietnam!*	Penguin, 1966
Halberstam, D.	*The Making of a Quagmire*	Bodley Head, 1965
Harvey, F.	*Air War in Vietnam*	Bantam, 1967
Herr, M.	*Dispatches*	Picador, 1978
Higgins, H.	*Vietnam*	Heinemann, 1975
Honey, P.	*Genesis of a Tragedy*	Ernest Benn, 1968
Karnov, S.	*Vietnam*	Century, 1983
Lifton, R.	*Home from the War*	Wildwood, 1974
Maclear, M.	*Vietnam*	Eyre Meethuen, 1981
McCarthy, M.	*The Seventeenth Degree*	Weidenfeld & Nicolson, 1967
McCarthy, M.	*Vietnam*	Penguin, 1968
Mullen, R.	*Blacks and Vietnam*	University Press, 1981
Papp, D.	*Vietnam*	McFarland, 1981
Powers, T.	*The War at Home*	Grossman, 1973
Ray, S. (ed.)	*Vietnam*	Nelson, 1966
Roy, J.	*The Battle of Dien Bien Phu*	Faber & Faber, 1965
Salisbury, H.	*Behind the Lines - Hanoi*	Secker & Warburg, 1967
Schlesinger, A.	*The Bitter Heritage*	Andre Deutsche, 1967
Sharp, U.	*Strategy for Defeat*	Presido, 1978
Sweezy, P. (ed.)	*Vietnam: The Endless War*	Monthly Review Press, 1970
Taber, R.	*The War of the Flea*	Paladin, 1970
Woodis, J. (ed.)	*Ho Chi Minh: Selected Works*	Lawrence & Wishart, 1969

Acknowledgements

Sources: (1) W.E. Garrett, "National Geographic", May, 1985 (2) Interview in the WGBH television documentary, "Vietnam: A Television History" (3) Martha Gellhorn, "Ladies' Home Journal", 1967 (4) Quoted in G. Emerson, "Winners and Losers", Random House, 1975 (5) Richard West, "The New Statesmen", April 25, 1975 (6) Joseph Buttinger, "A Dragon Defiant", David & Charles, 1972 (6) Interview with David Munro, "Observer Magazine", April, 1980 (8) John Kerry, Testimony to the US Senate Foreign Relations Committee, April 22, 1971. (9) S. Karnov, "Vietnam", Century Publishing, 1983 (10) T. Powers, "The War at Home", Grossman, 1973 (11) Interview in the BBC television documentary, "Haunted Heroes". (12) Quoted in M. Maclear's, "Vietnam: The Ten Thousand Day War", Eyre Methuen, 1981 (13) G. Emerson, "Winners and Losers", Random House, 1975 (14) Interview in the WGBH television documentary, "Vietnam: A Television History" (15) Interview in the BBC documentary, "Haunted Heroes" (16) Quoted in R. Lifton's, "Home from the War", Wildwood, 1974 (17) Quoted in, "Prevent the Crime of Silence", Allen Lane, 1971 (18) Seymour Hersh, "My Lai", Random House, 1970 (19) Philip Caputo, "A Rumour of War", Macmillan, 1977 (20) Colonel Robert Heinl, "Armed Forces Journal", June 7, 1971 (21) M. Gentleman, Vietnam and America, Grove Press, 1985 (22) M. Parris, "The American Film Industry and the Vietnam War", History Today, April, 1987 (23) Joel Swerdlow, "To Heal a Nation", Harper & Row, 1985.

Photographs: Black Star: p7; Edward Lansdale: p13; United Press International: p15, p23, p24, p47; Wide-World: p17, p29, p43; Camera Press: p26; British Film Institute: p57; DRV Information Dept: p38; Eupra Press: p52; Associated Press: p19, p33, p40, p42; National Geographic: p59; Establissment Cineatographique de Armees: p9; Network: p48.

The author would also like to thank Judith Simkin, Julia McGirr, Paul Waters, Michael Hickman, David Simkin, Peter Mansbridge and Peter Gibney for their help in the production of this book.